D1758728

The Little Book

of

Left-Right Equivalence

350 Mutual Blind Spots, Dueling
Hypocrisies, Double Flip-Flops and
Other Uncanny Parallels Between the
Two Tribes of Today's America

By Erik D'Amato

Illustrations by Zoltán Szécsi

Set in DTL Elzevir

Names: D'Amato, Erik, 1964— author.
Title: The little book of left-right equivalence : 350
mutual blind spots, dueling hypocrisies, double flip-flops
and other uncanny parallels between the two tribes of
today's America / Erik D'Amato.

ISBN 978-1-79-388194-6 (paperback)

First paperback edition March 2019

To all the good people on both sides

Politics, as a practice, whatever its professions, has always been the systematic organization of hatreds.

Henry Adams

———————

In all intellectual debates, both sides tend to be correct in what they affirm, and wrong in what they deny.

John Stuart Mill

Fig. I(a): A "MAGA" hat

Fig. I(b): A "pussy" hat

I

MAGA hats
═══════════
Pussy hats

Born again
═══════════
Woke

Social justice warriors

―――――――

The alt-right

The Tea Party

―――――――

Occupy

3

Regulation

===========

Law and order

Safe streets

===========

Safe spaces

Voter fraud

===========

Voter suppression

The Koch Brothers

========

George Soros

David Duke

========

Louis Farrakhan

Colin Kaepernick

========

Tim Tebow

Black lives matter

═══════════

Blue lives matter

Bread not bombs

═══════════

Jobs not mobs

The War on Women

═══════════

The War on Christmas

White supremacy
———
Cultural Marxism

Melting Pot
———
Sizzling Cauldron

Fig. II (a): Appalled by civil rights violations perpetrated by "fascist" Immigration and Customs Enforcement

Fig. II (b): Appalled by civil rights violations perpetrated by "fascist" Internal Revenue Service

II

Pretends to have a solution to the country's looming fiscal insolvency

———

Doesn't even bother pretending to have a solution to the country's looming fiscal insolvency

Doesn't even bother pretending to have a solution to climate change

———

Pretends to have a solution to climate change

Pretends to be outraged by the collapse
of the two-parent nuclear family

———

Doesn't even bother pretending to be outraged
by the collapse of the nuclear family

Doesn't even bother pretending to be outraged
by the growing domination of
politics by the super-rich

———

Pretends to be outraged by the growing
domination of politics by the super-rich

Is unconcerned with the environment,
but prefers to live surrounded by nature

———

Is very concerned with the environment,
but prefers to live surrounded by concrete

Thinks it's okay to change nature, but messing
with human biology is asking for trouble

———

Thinks it's okay to create GMO sex cyborgs,
but messing with nature is asking for trouble

Believes that bad weather is a sign of climate
change, but that a lack of bad weather doesn't
mean anything

———

Believes bad weather isn't a sign of climate
change, but that a lack of bad weather is proof
climate change is a hoax

Thinks that if Al Gore and other leading climate change activists live in mansions and fly private it's proof climate change is a hoax

━━━━━━━

Thinks that if leading climate change activists live in mansions and fly private it's okay to live in mansions and fly private, as long as you say the right things about climate change

Assumes that just because the most dire warnings about climate change haven't yet been borne out you can keep pumping greenhouse gases into the atmosphere forever

━━━━━━━

Assumes that just because the most dire warnings about inflation haven't yet been borne out you can keep printing money and pumping it into the economy forever

Belives that plug-in electric cars are "zero emission" vehicles, even if there is a coal-fired power plant on the other end of the plug

———

Believes "clean coal" is actually clean

Heard that road traffic is a sign of the inherent unsustainability of low-density living, but that a packed subway is a sign of a vibrant city

———

Heard that no one goes to the city anymore because it's too crowded

Knows there is a severe housing shortage, but tries to block all new residential construction or cripple it with burdensome regulations

———

Doesn't know there is a severe housing shortage, but thinks that if someone owns a piece of land in a residential neighborhood they should be able to quickly build an apartment block on it, and maybe a lead smelter out back

Supports "common sense" gun restrictions in the face of dogged opposition by the "extremist" National Rifle Association

---

Supports "common sense" abortion restrictions in the face of dogged opposition by "extremist" Planned Parenthood

Thinks there is a direct relationship between the number of guns in circulation and gun crime, even though the US has seen a huge drop in gun crime amid an unprecedented rise in the number of guns in circulation

---

Thinks there is an inverse relationship between the number of guns and gun crime, even though countries with the fewest guns in circulation also tend to have the lowest levels of gun crime

Boycotts sporting goods stores that don't
offer their customers assault rifles

━━━━━━━

Boycotts fast food chains that don't
offer their employees abortions

Believes it's a good idea to teach
schoolchildren how to handle guns

━━━━━━━

Believes it's a good idea to teach
schoolchildren how to handle genitals

Thinks the age of consent for getting an aspirin
from the school nurse should be higher than for
buying a French tickler at the drug store

━━━━━━━

Thinks it should be higher for
premarital sex than for marriage

Knows lots of people who actually believe abortion is murder, and that Americans would ever allow abortion to be outlawed nationwide

———

Knows lots of people who actually believe meat is murder, and that meat-eating might someday be outlawed anywhere

Considers it a moral necessity to save the lives of people who may have been improperly convicted of murder, but not healthy unborn children ready to pop out on their own

———

Considers it a moral necessity to stop unborn children from being killed, but not people who may have been improperly convicted of murder, who should be killed *right now*

Argues that society needs less coercive policing, but want more laws that need to be enforced

⸺

Argues that society needs fewer laws that need enforcing, but wants more coercive policing

Believes cops are racist killers, but that the state should have a monopoly on deadly force

⸺

Believes the police are a paragon of restraint, but that citizens should be armed against them

Appalled by civil rights violations perpetrated by "fascist" Immigration and Customs Enforcement agents

⸺

Appalled by civil rights violations perpetrated by "fascist" Internal Revenue Agency agents

Thinks the FBI used to be an elite force of comic book crime-fighting heroes brought to life, but is now the Democratic Party's own taxpayer-funded private militia

Thinks the FBI used to be a KGB-like shredder of civil liberties, but is now American democracy's first line of defense

Strongly believes in the rights of local and state governments, but that "sanctuary cities" defying federal immigration law should be occupied by the National Guard

Strongly believes "sanctuary cities" should be allowed to defy federal authority, but that if a city decided to ignore federal gun laws it should be razed by artillery fire

Thinks it's easy to ban guns but impossible to ban drugs, because someone will always find a way to smuggle them in or make them here

———

Thinks it's easy to ban drugs but impossible to ban guns, because someone will always find a way to smuggle them in or 3D print them here

Preoccupied by a relatively small number of murders committed with the AR-15 assault rifle

———

Preoccupied by a smaller number of murders committed by the MS-13 Latino crime gang

Loudly confident a wall on the Mexican border would work, but secretly fears it wouldn't

———

Loudly confident that a wall wouldn't work, but secretly fears it would

Says they are against a wall because it's wrong,
but are more interested in maintaining a steady
stream of cheap labor and future voters

========

Says they are for a wall because it's right,
but are more interested in maintaining a steady
stream of cheap labor and a good wedge issue

Willing to guarantee that among a large group
of refugees there are going to be some monsters

========

Willing to guarantee there won't be any

Thinks it isn't going too far to deny emergency
medical treatment to undocumented youths

========

Thinks it isn't going too far to offer them
in-state college tuition, as long as they can
prove they aren't US citizens from another state

Convinced that the vast majority of people in prison are there for non-violent drug offenses

———

Convinced that the vast majority are there for street crimes targeting innocent strangers

Believes the number of men falsely accused of sexual assault is way higher than it actually is

———

Believes it is way lower than it actually is

Wishes that accused sexual offenders could be convicted on a single uncorroborated allegation, especially if they are entitled white bros

———

Wishes that accused street criminals could be convicted on a single uncorroborated allegation, especially if they are disrespectful minorities

Thinks non-violent criminals shouldn't be incarcerated, except white bros or Republican political operatives, who should be frog-marched into jail without trial

———

Thinks violent criminals should be jailed for life, except members of right-wing militias occupying government installations, who should get reparations for being inconvenienced

Thinks incarceration should focus on punishment, except in cases of white-collar crime, where rehabilitation is key

———

Thinks incarceration should focus on rehabilitation, except in cases of white-collar crime, where savage restorative justice is key

Unconcerned that inmates in American prisons
are disproportionately minorities

Unconcerned that they are even more
disproportionately men

Unconcerned that women now vastly
outnumber men on college campuses

Unconcerned that men still vastly dominate
most fields in top universities

Unmoved by the hidden discrimination that
keeps black and Hispanic enrollment down in
elite universities

Unmoved by the open discrimination that
keeps Asian enrollment down

Believes college campuses are unsafe spaces for women because of an ongoing epidemic of rape and sexual assault, but would never seriously suggest they don't go

———

Believes college campuses are unsafe spaces for conservatives because of an epidemic of political correctness, but would never seriously suggest they don't go

Thinks it's okay for colleges to create separate dorms for different minority groups, but that the bathrooms in them should all be unisex

———

Thinks it's terrible for colleges to encourage self-segregation by minorities but that unisex bathrooms are asking for trouble, especially if you allow race-mixing in the dorms

Believes there can be free and open inquiry at a university where the most conservative member of the faculty is a liberal Democrat

———

Believes there can be free and open inquiry at a university run by Jerry Falwell, Jr.

Supports forcing colleges to hire more conservative professors, even though it would violate the principle of academic freedom

———

Supports firing professors who support gently urging colleges to hire more conservative professors, for daring to violate the principle of academic freedom

Wants the government to crack down on for-profit schools that leave students deeply in debt after obtaining vocational degrees of limited value on the job market

═══════════

Wants the government to crack down on liberal arts colleges that leave students even more deeply in debt after obtaining humanities degrees of no value on the job market

Loves American higher education for being so overwhelmingly progressive, without realizing that left-wing colleges and universities unwittingly constitute the country's most effective red-pilling operation

═══════════

Doesn't realize that America's overwhelmingly progressive institutions of higher education unwittingly act as the country's most effective red-pilling operation, even though they were red-pilled themselves while in college

Believes the academically gifted constitute a natural aristocracy but is skeptical of IQ

———

Believes IQ is easily measurable but is skeptical of academic overachievers

Believes the mentally disabled should be given world-class services, but if possible aborted

———

Believes the mentally disabled should be welcomed into the world as a gift from God, and then parked in front of the TV

Concerned that laws taking guns away from the mentally ill harm the rights of the disabled

———

Concerned that laws taking guns away from the mentally ill harm the rights of gun owners

Considers obese people aesthetically and morally challenging, but also thinks fat-shaming is bad, so is willing to give them a break

———

Considers fat people disgusting, but who isn't trying to lose a few pounds these days, so is willing to give them a break

Thinks that fighting obesity requires making difficult decisions, like forcing food retailers to stock more healthy options

———

Thinks that fighting obesity requires making difficult decisions, like treating fried chicken and waffles as two different meals

Doesn't believe adults should be free to decide for themselves whether to take the risks associated with smoking marijuana

═══════════

Doesn't believe they should be free to take the risks associated with drinking large sodas

Thinks people should be forced to bake gay wedding cakes, but not to serve in the military

═══════════

Thinks people should be forced to serve in the military, but not to bake gay wedding cakes

Considers requiring people on public assistance to work a modern form of slavery

═══════════

Considers requiring middle-class students to perform national service a modern form of slavery

Used to encourage people to question authority but now demands people respect expertise

———————

Used to demand people respect authority but now encourages people to question expertise

Thinks science has linked conservatism to a dangerous authoritarian personality disorder which may demand coercive inpatient psychiatric treatment

———————

Thinks liberals are the real authoritarians, and some day may need to be herded into camps for everyone's safety

Alarmingly uninterested in what the Founders were thinking while drafting the Constitution

━━━━━━━

Alarmingly fixated on what they were thinking

Certain that under the First Amendment burning the American flag is protected speech, but not hate speech

━━━━━━━

Certain that hate speech is protected speech, but not burning the flag

Doesn't find it unusual to spend an entire life without once flying the American flag

━━━━━━━

Doesn't find it unusual to spend every weekend driving around in a pickup truck flying a six-foot American flag

Considers the Hollywood blacklist of Communists in the 1950s one of the darkest moments in American history, but the "deplatforming" of rightwingers from social media no big deal

———

Considers the "deplatforming" of rightwingers one of the darkest moments in American history, but the Hollywood blacklist no big deal

Thinks it's terrible to get people fired by dredging up old social media posts of theirs that may be offensive, but if the other side does it will happily join in

———

Thinks it's fine to get people fired by dredging up old social media posts, but if the other side joins in it's just trolling

Circulates articles from obscure right-wing websites that are easily debunked

─────────

Circulates articles from obscure left-wing fact-checking websites that are easily debunked

Thinks posting terrible things about people they don't like makes them look virtuous

─────────

Thinks holding back a bit on the really off-color stuff makes them look virtuous

Wraps their right-wing views in ironic hyperbole, so if called out can pretend it's all sort of a harmless parody

─────────

Wraps their left-wing views in a blanket of earnestness so humorless it seems like a parody

Compulsively posts about how horrible
Republicans are, even though the only minds it
changes are a few fellow Democrats who get fed
up and become Republican trolls

═══════════

Compulsively trolls Democrat ex-friends

Snide comments

═══════════

ALL CAPS

Fig. III(a): Thinks Russia
used to be terrible but is
now not so bad

Fig. III(b): Thinks Russia is
now really terrible but used to
be not so bad

III

Pretends to be interested in world events
unrelated to the domestic political dramas they
obsess over 24/7

———

Doesn't even bother pretending to be interested
in world events unrelated to the domestic
political dramas they obsess over 24/7

Thinks Russia used to be terrible
but is now not so bad

———

Thinks Russia is now really terrible
but used to be not so bad

Thinks the best way to counter Russia's meddling in other countries' elections is by meddling in elections in other countries

———

Thinks Russia doesn't meddle in other countries' elections

After a few drinks will argue that Russia can't be blamed for wanting Crimea back

———

After a few drinks will argue that Mexico can't be blamed for wanting California back

Assumes that if an American president is popular in Western Europe or South America they are doing something wrong

———

Assumes that if an American president is popular in Eastern Europe or the American South they are doing something wrong

Thinks Israel used to be annoying
but is now fantastic, and American Jews are
insufficiently supportive of it

═══════════

Thinks Israel used to be fantastic
but is now annoying, and American Jews are
excessively supportive of it

Insists that anti-Zionism is inherently anti-
Semitic, but secretly has doubts

═══════════

Insists that anti-Zionism isn't inherently anti-
Semitic, but secretly has doubts

Insists Iran is okay but Saudi Arabia is terrible,
even though they are both bloodthirsty
theocracies that harbor anti-American terrorists

═══════════

Insists Iran is terrible but Saudi Arabia is okay,
at least for now

Believes Europe is way poorer and more
dangerous than it actually is

─────

Believes it is way richer and
safer than it actually is

Thinks the European Union is a genuine "post-
national" entity, rather than just a new, bigger
nation superimposed on a bunch of smaller
countries, like Germany after 1871

─────

Thinks the EU is a job-killing machine
staffed by woke dorks

Thinks the United Nations is democratic, even though Tuvalu gets the same vote as India, and France gets to veto anything it doesn't like

———

Thinks the United Nations is undemocratic, because it is run by foreigners and bans the use of nuclear weapons against civilian targets

Believes the inexorable rise of China poses an existential threat to the US, but that everything will probably turn out okay, because the US military retains force dominance in Asia

———

Believes everything will probably turn out okay with a rising China because the kids are doing well in Mandarin class

Really thinks it's time to move on from the whole Benghazi business

———

Really thinks it's time to move on from the whole missing Iraqi WMDs business

Considers the Islamist uprisings following the invasion of Iraq an unparalleled foreign policy blunder, but the Islamist uprisings following US support for the Arab Spring just bad luck

———

Considers the Islamist uprisings following the invasion of Iraq just bad luck, but the Islamist uprisings following the Arab Spring an unparalleled foreign policy blunder, because we already saw what happened after we ran into bad luck in Iraq

Thinks the CIA used to be American democracy's first line of defense, but is now a globalist shadow state

———

Thinks the CIA used to be a globalist shadow state, but is now the heroic FBI's first line of defense

Unable to see that the long-term detention of suspected terrorists without due process is an affront to America's core values

———

Able to see that the long-term detention of suspected terrorists without due process is an affront to America's values, but okay with it as long as they are in charge

Thinks America's global hegemony is probably bad for the world, but is okay with it because it's good for the American establishment

⎯⎯⎯⎯⎯

Thinks it's good for the world, but hates it because it's also good for the establishment

Used to "think globally, act locally" but now mostly thinks and acts nationally

⎯⎯⎯⎯⎯

Used to think nationally but now mostly thinks and acts anti-globally

Unconcerned by signs of populist-fueled "democratic backsliding" around the world

⎯⎯⎯⎯⎯

Concerned by "democratic backsliding," but also concerned that democracy may not be up to the job of forcing decisive coordinated global action on climate change

Used to see Edward Snowden as a heroic
Goliath-slaying David and Julian Assange
a rakish hacker rockstar, but now considers
Snowden a sad Putin stooge and Assange
a fat rapist Kremlin assassin

———

Used to consider Snowden a traitor and
Assange a greasy albino anarchist but now sees
Snowden as a misunderstood whistleblower
and Assange a Hillary-slaying Aryan sex god

Doesn't want corporations to collect any of
their personal data, but has no problem giving
the government a detailed record every April 15
about every penny they make, spend or save

———

Doesn't care if corporations put cameras in
their bathrooms, but thinks that automatic
voter registration is a government plot to gather
intel for mass gun confiscations

Used to think free trade and globalization were terrible and corrosive but now thinks they are natural and necessary

―――――――

Used to think free trade and globalization were natural and necessary but now thinks they are terrible and corrosive

Used to think multinational corporations were furnaces of neo-colonial exploitation but now thinks they provide critical funding for worthy global causes and a good place to work

―――――――

Used to think multinational corporations were a good place to work but now thinks they are job-killing machines run by foreigners and staffed by woke dorks

Sad when poor agricultural countries
industrialize because they become less colorful

═══════════

Sad when poor agricultural countries
industrialize because it means even more unfair
competition for US manufacturing

Unimpressed that the spread of capitalism has
helped cut extreme poverty in the developing
world by half since 1990, because the people
raised out of poverty are not all as rich as the
average American

═══════════

Unimpressed because many of them are now
richer than the average American

Concedes that Fidel Castro was a ruthless dictator, but argues that without him Cuba never would have achieved universal literacy

———

Concedes that Augusto Pinochet was a ruthless dictator, but argues that without him Chile woudn't be 10 times as rich as Cuba

Thinks that traditional societies in remoter parts of the Amazon jungle and elsewhere should be left alone, but that everyone else should be integrated with the West

———

Thinks that traditional societies in remoter parts of Europe should be protected from the corruptness of the West, but that other traditional socities should be dragged into modernity, especially if there are valuable natural resources under their ancestral lands

Considers inequality natural and necessary but elitism terrible and corrosive

———

Considers inequality terrible and corrosive but elitism natural and necessary

Reckons economic justice means less money for the rich and more money for the poor

———

Reckons it means less money for the professions and more money for the trades

Despite hating inequality is drawn to cutthroat "winner take all" industries and global cities with everything but a middle class

⸻

Despite not minding inequality is drawn to middlebrow industries and suburbs where everyone makes and lives basically the same

Doesn't know that income and wealth inequality is worst in the Blue states, even though they talk about inequality 24/7

⸻

Doesn't know, even though pointing it out would be an epic troll of the left

Reckons it may be time to start taxing churches, but that it would be unthinkable to strip hugely-endowed universities or big-money foundations of their tax exemptions

——————

Reckons it may be time to start taxing universities or big-money foundations, but that it would be unthinkable to strip churches of their tax exemptions

Supports other tax hikes, as long the country's urban centers of global innovation are spared

——————

Would be willing to go along, if it turned New York and San Francisco into Detroit circa 1983

Convinced that if you choose to invest your savings and are taxed on the resulting income it amounts to outrageous double taxation

═══════════

Convinced that if you choose to live in an area with sky-high taxes and property prices but can't fully write off your local taxes and mortgage interest it amounts to outrageous double taxation

Thinks an extra $1 in a taxpayer's pocket is a lot, as long as it involves a tax cut liberals hate

═══════════

Thinks it's a lot, as long as it involves a contraception benefit that conservatives hate

Believes poor whites are to blame for their plight, unlike members of other struggling communities, who are the victims of economic forces beyond their control

━━━━━━━━

Believes poor whites are the victims of economic forces beyond their control, unlike members of other struggling communities, who are to blame for their plight

Wary of programs to fight the decline in wages for low-skilled males because they might end up benefiting women or minorities

━━━━━━━━

Wary because they might end up only benefiting low-skilled white males

Appalled by the child poverty and inequality
linked to the growth of single-parent families,
but wary of funding programs to fight it

———

Wary of anyone who would be appalled by the
growth in single-parent families

Thinks unions can help raise the incomes of
lower-skilled workers by limiting uncontrolled
competition in the labor market, but that an
open door to labor from the Third World
doesn't have any impact on wages

———

Thinks immigration guts wages but unions are
fighting against the economic laws of gravity

Under the impression that per-person spending on public health programs like Medicare is lower in the US than in countries like Denmark

———————

Under the impression that Medicare isn't a government program

Says health care could be easily made affordable if you got rid of all the bureaucracy, but wouldn't actually do anything about it, because all that paper-shuffling represents millions of unionizable back-office jobs

———————

Agrees that health care could be easily made affordable if you got rid of all the bureaucracy, but also wouldn't do anything about it, because all that paper-shuffling represents billions in shareholder value

Unable to see that the return of robber baron-style monopoly capitalism is crushing wages, harming consumers and distorting democracy

———

Able to see it, but is okay with it as long as the robber barons are woke

Says it is obvious that socialism can work, it's just that it has never actually been tried

———

Says it is obvious the free market can work, it's just that it has never actually been tried

Believes that if democratic socialism came to the US it would be like Denmark, but with better ethnic restaurant options

═══════════

Believes that if democratic socialism came to the US it would be like Venezuela, but even poorer and more chaotic

Imagines Medicare for All being like a free version of the best private health care available now, instead of like Medicaid or a VA hospital

═══════════

Imagines Medicare for All being like a VA hospital in Venezuela

Unable to see that any functioning system of government benefits requires recipients to have responsibilities as well as rights

———

Able to see the need for a balance between responsibilities and rights, but only if it's the poor being held responsible

Unable to see that individualism and social diversity inevitably require a limited state and free markets

———

Unable to see that a limited state and free markets inevitably breed individualism and social diversity

Thinks you can have punishing taxes without talented individuals leaving for countries with better opportunities

———

Thinks you can have a competitive economy without being open to talented individuals from other countries

Isn't concerned that any attempt to build democratic socialism in America will quickly fail because of its deeply ingrained individualism and social diversity

———

Isn't reassured by the likelihood that any attempt to introduce democratic socialism into America will quickly fail

Sure that fiscal deficits are exclusively
caused by too much spending

═══════════

Sure they are caused by too little revenue

Certain that the national debt isn't
actually real money, but fiat currency
created from thin air is

═══════════

Certain that fiat currency isn't real money,
but the national debt is

Confident that in a national divorce the
Blue states would be helpless, even though they
have all the money

═══════════

Confident that in a national divorce the
Red states would be helpless, even though they
have all the food and fuel

Fig. IV(a): Actually thinks
Fox News is fair and balanced

Fig. IV(b): Actually thinks
CNN is fair and balanced

IV

Populists versus neoconservatives

———————

Populists versus neoliberals

Left-wing warhawks

———————

Right-wing peaceniks

Convinced the Democrats' biggest problem is
that they aren't hard enough on Republicans

———

Convinced the Republicans' biggest problem is
that they aren't hard enough on Democrats

Assumes that anyone who objects to even
the most ambitious parts of the Republicans'
agenda is a Democrat

———

Assumes that anyone who objects to even
the most ambitious parts of the Democrats'
agenda is a Republican

Thinks moderate congressional Republicans are heroes, unless they actually vote with Republicans, in which case they are monsters

———

Thinks moderate congressional Democrats are heroes, unless they actually vote with Democrats, in which case they are monsters

Says they wish Democrats would just nominate someone reasonable for president, even though the last time the party did they still called the candidate a crazed socialist

———

Says they wish Republicans would just nominate someone reasonable for president, even though the last time the party did they still called the candidate a right-wing extremist

Treats their potential Libertarian allies like disobedient children

———

Treats their potential Green Party allies like cheating spouses

Treats religious voters who identify as Democrats like pagan heretics

———

Treats minority voters who identify as Republicans like fugitive slaves

Doesn't understand why men might not be drawn to "the party of women"

———

Doesn't understand why women might not be drawn to a party of unemployed wife-beaters

Falls in love with candidates

———

Falls in line behind candidates

Believes dynasticism is bad but keeps voting for
Kennedys, Clintons, Browns and Cuomos

———

Believes dynasticism isn't necessarily bad but
gave up after a couple of Bushes

Used to think politicians should be free to
carouse like rock stars but now demands they be
as chaste as 1950s TV parents

———

Used to demand politicians be as chaste as
1950s TV parents but now thinks they should
be free to carouse like gangster rap stars

Thinks it's okay for politicians to lie as long as they do so in an ostentatiously cerebral manner

═══════════

Thinks it's okay as long as they do so in an ostentatiously folksy manner

Reckons that if your politics are upright enough you can personally be as dishonest and disreputable as you want

═══════════

Reckons that being as personally dishonest and disreputable as you want is a good political strategy

Willing to support a billionaire for president as long as he acts like a barfly and may be broke

———

Willing to support a billionaire as long as he acts like a bicycle-riding Scandinavian monarch and could buy out Denmark

Gives money to Democratic candidates in states they've never visited but doesn't know the name of their own state representative

———

Keeps their political donations local and knows their state representative, because he came around asking for help in gerrymandering the state's Democrats into oblivion

Beholden to well-connected oil companies that pollute while creating energy

———

Beholden to well-connected green energy firms that don't pollute while not creating energy

Most reliable and enthusiastic partisans used to be affluent Victorian women fixated on controlling ill-mannered lower caste men

———

Most reliable and enthusiastic partisans are affluent neo-Victorian women fixated on controlling ill-mannered lower caste men

Lorded over by a small but powerful group of far-right white Christians

———

Lorded over by a small but powerful group of far-left Jewish athiests

Heartened by the support of countless A-list
stars of film, television and stage

———————

Heartened by the support of a handful of B-list
entertainers, including two presidents

Thinks Kanye West should steer clear of
politics and focus on getting right with Kim

———————

Thinks Taylor Swift should steer clear of
politics and focus on getting right with God

Shocked when Trump welcomed Kanye
to the White House

———————

Shocked when Obama welcomed Ludacris
and Pusha T to the White House

Believes Obama can claim credit for the economic uptick which started just a few months into his presidency

———

Believes Trump can claim credit for the uptick which started a few minutes into his presidency

Convinced Ronald Reagan won the Cold War without the help of the Democrats who controlled Congress for most of his presidency

———

Convinced Bill Clinton balanced the federal budget without the help of the Republicans who controlled Congress for most of his presidency

Doesn't want anyone to know Massachusetts has a popular Republican governor, because it makes Republicans look sensible

―――――

Doesn't want anyone to know, because it makes Massachusetts look sensible

Doesn't want anyone to know that Vermont has among the least restrictive gun laws in America, because it makes guns look sensible

―――――

Doesn't want anyone to know, because it makes Bernie Sanders look sensible

Doesn't want anyone to know that Dick Cheney was in favor of same-sex marriage before Barack Obama, because it makes Obama look bad

―――――

Doesn't want anyone to know, because it makes Cheney look bad

Doesn't want anyone to know that Bill Clinton
supported a crackdown on illegal immigrants

———

Doesn't want anyone to know that Reagan and
both Bushes supported amnesty

Doesn't want anyone to know both Clintons
promised to "Make America Great Again"

———

Doesn't want anyone to know the Clintons
were MAGA before Trump was

Doesn't want anyone to know Trump invited
the Clintons to his wedding

———

Doesn't want anyone to know that they came,
and had a tremendous time

Willing to forgive a politician for wearing
blackface, if it was a long time ago

———

Willing to forgive them, if it was a long time
ago and they are a Democrat

Still sure Obama is a secret Muslim

———

Still sure Trump is a secret Russian

Still sure there is a smoking gun hidden in
Trump's unreleased tax returns

———

Still sure there is a smoking gun hidden in
Obama's unreleased college transcripts

Can't quite believe Ruth Bader Ginsburg was
best friends with Antonin Scalia,
because he seems so evil

===========

Can't quite believe it,
because she seems so evil

Has a soft spot for Nixon, because he expanded
government in ways that enraged conservatives

===========

Has a soft spot for Nixon, because he
enraged liberals even more

Thinks George W. Bush was a pretty good
president but is a terrible artist

===========

Thinks George W. Bush was a terrible
president but is a pretty good artist

Actually thinks Fox News is fair and balanced

———

Actually thinks CNN is fair and balanced

Actually thinks the "Borowitz Report"
is real news, or funny satire

———

Actually thinks the "Babylon Bee"
is real news, or funny satire

Aggrieved that *The New York Times* gets away
with printing endless articles mocking and
deriding Trump-supporting white heartlanders

———

Aggrieved that the *Times* features the
occasional sympathetic portrait of Trump-
supporting white heartlanders

Lazily claims most mainstream journalists are leftists, when in reality they tend to be a narrow type of professional-class neoliberal

―――――

Lazily claims most mainstream journalists have no political leanings

Willing to believe that if the mainstream media publishes a story that is bad for Republicans it's fake news, even if it turns out to be totally true

―――――

Willing to believe that nothing is fake news if it's damaging enough to Republicans

Thinks media organizations need to be racially diverse, but that calls for "viewpoint diversity" in the newsroom are just right-wing trolling

―――――

Thinks diversity in media means a token right-wing minority talking head or two

Unable to see that calling the media the "enemy of the people" is dangerous and un-American

━━━━━━

Able to see it is dangerous and un-American, but totally okay doing it to Fox News

Wishes they had access to a nationwide network of commercially successful talk radio stations

━━━━━━

Wishes they had access to a nationwide network of government-funded public radio stations

Thinks American presidential elections can be thrown by a few dozen media manipulation experts working for the GRU and SVR

━━━━━━

Thinks elections can be thrown by a few dozen media manipulation experts working for Think Progress and Teen Vogue

Criticizes media outlets for employing armies of millennial progressive crusaders but then doesn't give the same outlets credit when the woke propagandists are laid off en masse

―――――

Criticizes media outlets for laying off millennial progressive crusaders but then doesn't give the same outlets credit for continuing to be mostly staffed by woke propagandists

Assumes that algorithms and artificial intelligence are inherently biased because they are built by people, and people all have their own natural biases, but also that prestige media outlets aren't similarly hobbled by inherent bias

―――――

Assumes that the news is inherently biased because it is made by liberals, but algorithms which end up denying bail or mortgages to minorities are just following the data

Masterful at spreading their political messages via church pulpits

———

Masterful at spreading their political messages via the social media accounts of #Brands

Aggrieved that the left's relative dominance of American culture doesn't translate into dominance of American political institutions

———

Aggrieved that the right's political dominance doesn't translate into cultural dominance

Accuses the country's liberal elite of living in a cultural bubble, even though it largely resides in global cities of unparalleled diversity

———

Accuses people in the heartland of living in a cultural bubble, even though most of the media and cultural product heartlanders consume is created by coastal elites

Doesn't think it's odd that some of the same male senators who dominated the hearings into allegations of sexual misconduct against Clarence Thomas dominated the Brett Kavanaugh hearings 27 years later

———

Doesn't think it's odd that Al Franken played a member of the Judiciary Committee in a 1991 "Saturday Night Live" skit about the Thomas hearings and then went on to become a Senator and a member of the same committee, until being forced to resign over sexual misconduct

Doesn't think it's odd that five years later people would still be talking about Obama's ugly tan suit from 2014

———

Doesn't think it's odd that 35 years later people would still be talking about Reagan's ugly brown suit from 1983

Thinks the Electoral College is unrepresentative, because it dilutes the votes of large states like New York

———

Thinks it isn't unrepresentative enough, because the 2016 presidential election was between two New Yorkers

Thinks the Senate is unrepresentative, even though its weighting of votes is way fairer than that of the UN

———

Thinks the Senate is nicely representative, because after a few years even senators from the North end up talking like Southern gentlemen

Thinks preserving the rule of law is of such vital importance there may be no option but to pack the Supreme Court with unfliching Democrats

———

Thinks preserving the rule of law is of such vital importance there may be no option but to shell the Supreme Court into rubble

Unable to see that the long-running concentration of power at the federal level is distorting and poisoning American politics, no matter who is in charge

———

Able to see, but totally okay with it as long as they are in charge

Winces when they remember how they use to talk about "draining the swamp"

Winces when they remember how they use to talk about "smashing the state"

Says policies should be made "for the children" but has no children

---

Has lots of children but thinks "for the children" sounds bad for kids

Says policies should be made "for the nation" but has always hated nationalism

---

Says policies should be made "for the nation" but has always hated the federal government

Accuses Democrats of bamboozling working-class voters with bogus class war rhetoric

———

Accuses Republicans of bamboozling working-class voters with bogus culture war rhetoric, and tries to buttress their case with the bogus term "false consciousness"

Exhilarated by a growing "age gap" in party preference, without realizing that as people get old they get more conservative, and someday soon the average voter will be 60

———

Terrified by a growing "age gap" in party preference, without realizing that as people get old they get more conservative, and someday soon the average voter will be 60

Would happily write a book about how
ashamed they are of being a Democrat, but is
afraid of being expelled from polite society

———

Would happily write a book about how
ashamed they are of being a Republican, but the
market is already saturated

Doesn't see that all the political correctness will
eventually destroy the Democratic Party

———

Doesn't see that all the political incorrectness
has already destroyed the Republican Party

Thinks that Trump represents an unprecedented threat to democracy, as opposed to just another trash-talking populist plutocrat like Silvio Berlusconi or Ross Perot

———

Thinks that Trump represents an unprecedented expression of democracy, as opposed to just another trash-talking populist

Expresses their opposition to Trump's vulgarity with vulgarisms coarser than Trump's

———

Expresses their support for Trump's vulgarity with still even coarser vulgarisms

Still doesn't see that the quickest
and easiest way to "normalize" Trump is to act
as crude, hyperbolic and erratic as he does

========

Still doesn't see anything abnormal about
Trump's presidency

Used to think there was a far left but doesn't
anymore, because the media only talks
about the "far right"

========

Used to think there was a far right but doesn't
anymore, because it's unfair the media never
talks about the "far left"

Thinks they are right-wing even though their most right-wing positions were considered left-wing until five minutes ago

―――――

Thinks they are left-wing even though the people they hate most for being right-wing are poorer than them

Doesn't understand that no matter how much you hate people for being right-wing, there will always be people who hate you for not being left-wing enough

―――――

Doesn't understand that no matter how much you hate people for being left-wing, there will always be people who hate you for not being right-wing enough, and they are probably armed and dangerous

Assumes that anyone who spends their entire life hanging out with liberals but who insists they aren't a liberal is probably joking

———————

Assumes that anyone who spends their entire life hanging out with conservatives but who insists they aren't one is probably looking for BDSM hookups

Afraid that if their left-wing views are found out at work their co-workers might beat them up

———————

Afraid that if their right-wing views are found out at work their co-workers might get them fired and driven from their industry for life

Confident that chasing politicians out of restaurants is democracy in action, but yelling abuse at journalists covering political rallies is a chilling breach of civic norms

━━━━━━

Confident that chasing politicians out of restaurants is a chilling breach of civic norms, but yelling abuse at journalists covering political rallies is democracy in action

Thinks a dozen bombs sent to prominent Democrats is a shocking act of political terrorism, but the shooting up of the congressional Republican baseball team is just one of those things

━━━━━━

Thinks the shooting up of the Republican baseball team is a shocking act of political terrorism, but a dozen bombs sent to Democrats is just one of those things

First response to news of a mass shooting
or terror attack is desperate hope it was
perpetrated by white nationalists

———

First response is desperate hope it was
perpetrated by radical Islamists

Believes that when fascism comes to America it
will be wrapped in the flag and carrying a cross

———

Believes that when fascism comes to America it
will be under the guise of anti-fascism

Thinks the idea of American Exceptionalism
is dopey but amazed the US might follow the
world in adopting European-style populism

———

Thinks the idea of American Exceptionalism
is great but happy to join the world in adopting
European-style populism

Perpetually convinced the Democrats are just one election away from an enduring majority, which would free them from ever again having to compromise with Republicans

═══════════

Perpetually convinced the Republicans are just one election away from being able to gerrymander the Democrats into oblivion once and for all

Vows that if Republicans win the next election they'll move to Denmark or some other place they don't realize happens to be among the whitest spots on Earth

═══════════

Vows that if Democrats win they'll move to Idaho or some other place they know is so white it would make Denmark look like Djibouti

Fig. V(a): Terrified by images
of women wearing hijabs

Fig. V(b): Terrified by images
of women wearing bonnets

V

Thinks immigrants used to be great but are
now drug-smuggling rapists

═══════════

Thinks working-class whites used to be great
but are now meth-addled racists

Convinced America is turning into a Third
World country, and really angry about it

═══════════

Convinced America is turning into a Third
World country, and really happy about it

Angry that Italian-Americans and other "white ethnics" have forgotten how they used to be treated like Latinos

———

Happy that white ethnics have forgotten how they used to be treated like Latinos

Thinks white ethnics are turning into the worst kind of white people

———

Thinks white ethnics are turning into the best kind of almost totally white people

Doesn't worry that Latinos may turn out like other white ethnics, despite how terrible it would be for their electoral prospects

———

Doesn't worry that Latinos might not turn out like other white ethnics, despite how terrible it would be for their electoral prospects

Sad that the native peoples of North Americans were displaced by outsiders

———————

Angry that the native peoples of Europe are being displaced by outsiders

Angry that anyone would use the word "native" or "indigenous" or "peoples" to describe Europeans or Americans of European descent

———————

Happy that many Native Americans agree "indigenous Europeans" is an objective term

Shares memes casting the Pilgrims as illegal aliens without realizing it makes unrestricted immigration look like national suicide

———————

Re-shares the same memes without realizing it makes anyone except Native Americans who argue against unrestricted immigration look like idiot hypocrites

Says Columbus Day should be abolished because it makes Native Americans feel bad, but secretly fears losing a long weekend during peak New England fall foliage season

---

Secretly hopes Columbus Day is abolished, because it will make Italian-Americans Republicans for life, but also fears losing a long weekend during peak fall college football season

Thinks it's okay for Native American tribes to use DNA tests to establish tribal membership, but if any other country grants citizenship based on genetics it's Nazism pure and simple

---

Thinks it's okay for Native American tribes to use DNA tests, as long as it keeps the Elizabeth Warren "Fauxcahontas" meme alive

Prefers "illegal alien" but will settle
for "illegal immigrant"

======

Will settle for "undocumented immigrant"
but prefers "New American"

Doesn't know what to call people who are born
in Africa and emigrate to America, but is pretty
sure it's not just "African-Americans"

======

Also doesn't know what to call them, but is
pretty sure it's not just "Americans"

Unashamed to argue that the US would be
stronger if everyone living in the country
illegally was summarily deported

======

Unashamed to argue that the US would be
stronger if it deported white "deplorables" to
make room for harder-working New Americans

Thinks anyone who migrates to the US is instantly 100% American, especially if they are poor and inclined to vote Democratic

———————

Thinks it takes a lifetime for immigrants to become true Americans, unless they are rich and inclined to vote Republican

Believes that dual citizenship means you can be 100% American and at the same time a full citizen of any number of other countries

———————

Believes you can be a 100% American and a full citizen of another country, but only if the Old Country is in Europe and the EU and George Soros are waging white genocide against it

Hates the people who put up "Hate Has No Home Here" signs in their front yards

———

Loves that the people they hate hate the "Hate Has No Home Here" sign they put up

Terrified by images of women wearing hijabs

———

Terrified by images of women wearing handmaids' bonnets

Okay with the intermarriage of native-born whites and recent immigrants, as long as they keep it quiet and the kids learn to speak English

———

Okay with the intermarriage of WASPs and Jews, as long as the wedding makes the society pages and the kids learn to speak Hebrew

Thinks non-Hispanic whites are justified in worrying about becoming minorities in their own country, while denying that other minorities have anything to worry about

========

Thinks non-Hispanic whites are silly for worrying about becoming minorities in their own country, while constantly talking about how bad it is to be a minority in the US

Believes overpopulation is a problem, but that sharply higher levels of immigration from the developing world are needed to offset demographic decline in the West

========

Believes overpopulation isn't a problem, but that there wouldn't be a need for immigrants even if Europe or the US were down to their last arkload of human breeding pairs

Pretty sure that chattel slavery was invented by European Christians, even though it was approvingly mentioned in the Koran hundreds of years before the era of European colonialism

———

Pretty sure it was invented by Arab Muslims, even though it was approvingly mentioned in the Old Testament a thousand years before the Koran was written

Surprised that North America was responsible for only a small portion of the Atlantic slave trade, because Anglo settlers seemed so cruel

———

Surprised, because it seems like the Anglo settlers would have had it much more together than the Spanish and Portugese

Thinks that having black actors play the
Founding Fathers is a little weird

═══════════

Thinks white actors playing black
characters is racist

Believes white musicians playing black music is
cultural appropriation

═══════════

Believes there's nothing black about Elvis

Doesn't see that concern about cultural
appropriation isn't necessarily "anti-white"

═══════════

Doesn't see that concern about cultural
appropriation is the whitest thing since the
Donny & Marie Osmond show

Assumes that, unlike with gender, you can't just
self-identify as belonging to another race

———

Assumes that you can choose whatever race you
want to identify with, at least if there is a liberal
around that it will make angry or confused

Assumes that if someone is of mixed white and
black ancestry they are actually just black

———

Also assumes they are actually just black,
or maybe a quadroon

Assumes "white power" and "black power" or
"white privilege" and "Jewish privilege" are
somehow equivalent

———

Assumes there are no similarities

Doesn't even bother pretending to be opposed
to segregation in their area's public schools

———

Pretends to be opposed to segregation
in their area's public schools

Thinks that an increasingly diverse society can
still be led by a handful of privileged white men

———

Thinks that an increasingly diverse society can
be led by a handful of privileged white women

Thinks white men are terrible, but idealizes
Northern European feminist males, who are
basically the whitest men on the planet

———

Thinks white men are great, just a little soft

Lives in a linguistic bubble, only speaking English and surrounded by people who can only speak English

———

Lives in a linguistic bubble, only speaking English and surrounded by people who can only speak languages other than English

Reckons that if South Africa can have 12 official languages the US can certainly have two

———

Reckons that if English was good enough for the Twelve Apostles it's good enough for everyone in America

Assumes that if a town is 50% black and 50% Latino everyone is certain to get along just fine

———

Assumes that if a town is 50% black and 50% Latino you should immediately dial 911

Assumes economically struggling macho minority men have more in common with effete affluent liberal white women than with economically struggling macho white men

———

Assumes economically struggling macho white men have more in common with effete affluent conservative white men than with economically struggling macho minority men

Finds it understandable that marginalized black communities would vote for fiery leaders like Marion Barry who promise to stick it to the man, even if they make their supporters' lives objectively worse

———

Finds it understandable that marginalized white communities would vote for fiery leaders like Donald Trump who promise to stick it to the man, even if they make their supporters' lives objectively worse

Thinks that if a well-publicized hate crime is revealed as a hoax the focus should remain on the "larger truths" of the case

=====

Thinks that if a hate crime is revealed as a hoax the larger truth is that hate crimes don't exist

Can't understand that encouraging non-white people to wallow 24/7 in their racial grievances inevitably leads to more white racism

=====

Can't understand why non-white people would have any reason to be aggrieved

Thinks multiculturalism is hard because people with different values can never live cheek-to-cheek without tension or misunderstandings

=====

Thinks multiculturalism is easy because people with different tastes can live cheek-to-cheek without tension or misunderstandings

Has never considered that wokeness mirrors racism in allowing mediocre individuals from in-groups to limit their exposure to economic and social competition from members of artifically-created out-groups

========

Has never considered that racism shelters mediocre individuals from economic and social competition

Doesn't see that the entire Red-Blue split is an example of the inherent weaknesses of multiculturalism, even though they talk about multiculturalism 24/7

========

Doesn't see it, even though pointing it out would be the most epic troll of the left imaginable

Fig. VI(a): Troubled by gentrification but can't live without all the luxuries it makes possible

Fig. VI(b): Troubled by immigration but can't live without all the bargains it makes possible

VI

Countryside and also some
city (usually the best parts)
but mostly the suburbs

———

Cities and also some
countryside (usually the best parts)
but mostly the suburbs

Mansions, apartments, one-family houses,
run-down housing projects

———

McMansions, garden apartments,
one-family houses, run-down shacks

Backyard chicken coops,
cute little goats
and rabbits (pets)

═══════════

Backyard chicken coops,
cute little goats
and rabbits (meat)

Has a black housekeeper
that is "just like family"

═══════════

Has a European au pair
that is "just like family"

Comfortable dodging used
shotgun shells and cow pies

━━━━━━━━━

Comfortable dodging used
syringes and hobo shit

Tempted to simplify their lives and save
some money by getting one of those stylish
new $175,000, 200-square foot "tiny houses"

━━━━━━━━━

Tempted by those stylish new $45,000,
400-square foot single-wide mobile homes

Public transit, ride-hailing
apps, bike shares

━━━━━━━━━

Cars, trucks, heavy-duty
mobility scooters

Trucker hats and tattoos,
Pabst Blue Ribbon, Frito pie, Edison bulbs and
reclaimed barn wood, Bob Ross (ironic)

═══════════

Trucker hats and tattoos,
Pabst Blue Ribbon, Frito pie, Edison bulbs and
reclaimed barn wood, Bob Ross (unironic)

Factory, bartender, babysitter

═══════════

Maker space, mixologist, caregiver

Made in USA

═══════════

Handcrafted with Brooklyn pride

TV dinner, Carl's Jr.,
Chick-fil-A, Waffle House

═══════════

Meal kit, Shake Shack, juniper-brined baby
chicken, waffle-cut heritage potato fries

Bone broth, kale, avocado toast,
guacamole with peas, Sub-Zero Pro

═══════════

Bouillon cube soup, collards,
grilled pimento cheese, frozen peas and corn,
avocado-colored Frigidaire

Loves South American "churrascaria" steakhouses, but can never remember how to pronounce "churrascaria"

═══════════

Loves the Andean "supergrain" quinoa, and wants everyone to know it's pronounced "KEEN-wah"

Wouldn't eat Filipino "Kari Kari" beef stew, because beef with peanut butter is gross

═══════════

Wouldn't eat it, because the beef probably wasn't free range, nuts contain deadly toxins, and eating it might be cultural appropriation, even if even if you know it's pronounced "KARE-KARE"

Target, T.J. Maxx,
Eileen Fisher, Stitch Fix

━━━━━━━━━

Walmart, Marshalls,
Lilly Pulitzer, QVC

InStyle

━━━━━━━━━

Sunday Styles

Muffin top, Paleo

━━━━━━━━━

Thigh gap, Keto

Troubled by gentrification but can't live without
all the luxuries it makes possible

———————

Troubled by immigration but can't live without
all the bargains it makes possible

Doesn't think it's insane to spend $1,000 on a
pair of dogs to go hunting with once a year

———————

Doesn't think it's insane to spend $10,000 on
a pair of new knees for a dog, even though it
normally gets around in a handbag

Never wonders how a glass of Grüner Veltliner
can cost the same as a pair of Old Navy chinos

———————

Wonders why India Pale Ale costs
so much, and why America even has to
import beer from India

Unashamed to never travel outside
of the United States

———

Unashamed to never travel outside
of a few places on the coasts

Unashamed to use climate-destroying
motor vehicles to take enjoyable but
unnecessary trips

———

Unashamed to use climate-destroying
airplanes to take enjoyable but
unnecessary trips

Pretends to love vacations "roughing it" in the Third World but in reality would prefer to go hobnob on Martha's Vineyard

———

Pretends to love vacations "roughing it" in the American West but in reality would prefer to go hobnob on Hilton Head

Values "authenticity," to a point

———

Values "authenticity" tremendously, but also heard it can mask a form of white supremacy

Doesn't see the soul-crushing uniformity of the chain restaurants and stores they like

———

Doesn't see that due to globalization the exact same barnwood- and Edison bulb-stuffed hipster restaurants and stores they like are now everywhere from Times Square to Timbuktu

Says they love Grand Ole Opry but would
rather listen to Billy Ray Cyrus

———————

Says they love opera but would
rather listen to Miley Cyrus

Orange is the New Black,
Will & Grace, Antiques Roadshow

———————

NCIS, Duck Dynasty, Pawn Stars

Wakanda

———————

Narnia

Hates off-color or politically incorrect
comedy, even if it's really funny

———

Loves it, even if it's really unfunny

Against modern "participation trophy" culture
where everyone is treated like a winner even if
they are barely competitive, or a total loser

———

Against modern "instant publishing" culture
where anyone can put out a book without going
through traditional editorial gatekeepers

Western saddle, "charity ball"

———

English saddle, "gala fundraiser"

Scientists, architects, gardeners,
flight attendants, teachers, day care workers,
lawyers, street criminals

———

Engineers, homebuilders, farmers,
pilots, firefighters, exterminators,
cops, white-collar criminals

Research fellowships,
internships, flextime

———

Religious fellowships,
summer jobs, overtime

Most of the people who
serve in the military

───────────

Most of the civilians who
control the military

Most of the people who
make luxury goods

───────────

Most of the people who
buy luxury goods

Sales

───────────

Development

STEM, GED

————

STEAM, TED

The "Intellectual Dark Web"

————

All other intellectuals

Goes to fancy dinner parties but doesn't know which one is the salad fork

———————

Wrote dissertation on table settings in 18th-Century France, but lives on ramen

Has a Ph.D. in the theory of class conflict, but doesn't realize it's in the upper one

———————

Thinks "class conflict" is something that happens on a school playground, but knows it isn't in the upper one

Thinks it "takes a village" to raise children,
but lives in a city

———

Lives in a village, but thinks it only takes a
family to raise children

Would prefer to send their kids
to public school, but it's just too risky

———

Would prefer to send them to private school,
but it's just too expensive

Helicoptering, latchkey,
intervention, screentime

———

Chores, backyard,
spanking, screentime

Worried that home wi-fi signals
may cause cancer

═══════════

Worried that fluoride in municipal water
impurifies precious bodily fluids

Thinks that if someone goes to a
psychotherapist it's evidence they are insane

═══════════

Thinks it's evidence they are sane

Ayahuasca, weed, Ambien, sleep

═══════════

Oxycontin, meth, Fentanyl, death

Fig. VII(a): Thinks Jesus was an important philosopher, even though no serious philophers do

Fig. VII(b): Thinks Žižek is an important philosopher, even though no serious philosophers do

VII

Christianity > Judiasm >
Agnosticism > New Age > Islam

=========

Agnosticism > New Age >
Judiasm > Islam > Christianity

Non-denominational megachurch > Baptist >
Catholic > Methodist > Mormon > Episcopal,
Presbyterian and other liberal denominations
mostly concerned about making sure the old
church building is tastefully renovated

=========

Unitarian > Episcopal/Presbyterian (nice
church building) > Episcopal/Presbyterian (bad
building) > Catholic (guitar) > Catholic (organ)
> your pick of racist snake-handlers

Society for Ethical Culture > Reform >
Conservative > Orthodox > Jews for Jesus

━━━━━━━

Jews for Jesus > Orthodox > Conservative >
Reform > Society for Ethical Culture

Gloats about being among the lucky few
to go to Heaven

━━━━━━━

Gloats about being among the lucky few
to go to "Hamilton"

Confident they have all the answers because
they occasionally read shared Bible verses

═══════════

Confident because they occasionally read
shared Vox.com "explainers"

Was willing to give the Catholic Church a pass
on the sexual abuse scandal until it became
clear the Vatican is run by a gay mafia more
concerned with climate change than religion

═══════════

Is willing to give the Catholic Church a pass,
now that it has become clear the Vatican is run
by a gay mafia more concerned with climate
change than religion

Thinks Christian Science is
related to actual science

════════════

Thinks the social sciences are
related to actual science

Thinks Jesus Christ was an important
philosopher, even though no serious
philosophers do

════════════

Thinks Slavoj Žižek is an important
philosopher, even though no serious
philosophers do

Belives wine can literally be blood

════════════

Belives words can literally be violence

Considers it a national emergency when
Starbucks doesn't use Christmas-themed cups

———————

Considers it a national emergency when
Starbucks uses them

Against mixing religion and politics
because it's bad for politics

———————

Against mixing religion and politics
because it's bad for religion

Thinks it's in bad taste to criticize the Pope for
being an absolute monarch who exists to mix
religion and politics

———————

Thinks it's in bad taste to criticize the Dalai
Lama for being an absolute monarch who exists
to mix religion and politics

Doesn't want anyone to know that Jesus was a Jewish migrant socialist activist

———

Doesn't want anyone to know that Hitler was an anti-Christian anti-smoking vegetarian animal rights activist

Doesn't want anyone to know that Christmas is a recycled pagan celebration that was outlawed by the Pilgrims

———

Doesn't want anyone to know that the creator of Kwanzaa was convicted of torturing women with a soldering iron

Believes God was plenty clear that He was
making Adam and Eve, not Adam and Steve

════════

Believes the story of creation is sexist BS, plus
Gaia created the universe by pegging Uranus

Can't believe that Hillary Clinton is a devout
Christian, because she seems so educated

════════

Can't believe it, because she seems so evil

Wants sinners who repent and become dutiful
Christians to be given redemption and a chance
to have their souls saved

════════

Wants sinners who repent and become dutiful
Democrats to be given a regular column and
slot on TV posing as a Republican

Okay having schoolchildren spend time
learning about creationism
rather than actual science

⎯⎯⎯⎯

Okay having them spend time
learning about pioneering women scientists
rather than actual science

Thinks science can tell you everything
about animals except how long they've been
around on Earth, for which you need
to consult scripture

⎯⎯⎯⎯

Thinks science can tell you everything
about animals except what sex they are, which
you can only find out by asking them

Believes that animals need to live uncaged and free to follow their instincts, but that humans are better off in heavily-engineered societies

========

Believes that God made humans so they would not live like animals

Doesn't want anyone to appreciate how well members of America's unimaginably diverse religious patchwork get along amid an increasingly bitter and rigid national political discourse, because it makes religion look more sensible and healthy than secular politics

========

Doesn't want anyone to appreciate it, because it makes it look like multiculturalism is working

Denies that their burning political tribalism is a replacement for religion, because they don't consider themselves religious

═══════════

Denies it, because they still consider themselves religious

Used to strongly believe that human values are a changeable and sometimes random social construction designed to cement social hierarchies, but now strongly believes they are eternal, universal and unquestionable truths

═══════════

Used to strongly believe in values

Fig. VIII(a): Right-wing "incels" who
blame left-wing women for the fact
that they are involuntarily celibate

Fig. VIII(b): Left-wing incels who
blame right-wing incels for the fact
that they are involuntarily celibate

VIII

Believes sex is just for recreation,
but never seems to have any

═══════════

Believes sex is just for procreation,
but seems to have it all the time

Prefers M/F, but will settle for LGBT

═══════════

Prefers LGBTQIAPK, but will
settle for LGBTQ

Thinks polyamory can be an acceptable lifestyle, but only if it is subverting the patriarchy

———

Thinks it can be an acceptable lifestyle, but only if it is upholding the patriarchy

Considers pornography to be disgraceful exploitation, but thinks that prostitution should be called "sex work" and treated like any other highly-skilled profession

———

Considers prostitution to be disgraceful exploitation, but thinks that pornography is a forgivable sin, as long as it's straight and no animals or people you know are in it

Less concerned by the collapse in marriage rates than in promoting same-sex marriage

———————

Less concerned by the collapse in marriage rates than in preventing same-sex marriage

Thinks sodomy should be discouraged because of the offhand chance straights will give it a try and end up thinking they are gay

———————

Thinks "conversion therapy" should be banned because of the offhand chance gays will give it a try and end up thinking they are straight

Outraged when a man decides to take a
woman's first name

═══════════

Outraged when a woman decides to take a
man's last name

Constantly says bad things about penises

═══════════

Has never once spoken the word "vagina"

Thinks it's acceptable to call women "bitches"

═══════════

Thinks it's acceptable to call women "bitches,"
as long as it's other women or gay men
appropriating the slur in a self-affirming way,
or black rappers, at least for the time being

Professes support for gender equality but secretly wants the man to be the breadwinner while the woman stays home with the kids

===========

Secretly wants the woman to be the bread-winner, while the man stays home with the cats

Thinks society should encourage women to be stay-at-home moms, except "welfare mothers," who should be pushed into the workforce

===========

Thinks unemployed single mothers should be given better benefits and services, but married stay-at-home moms shamed into working

Doesn't think men can ever play an equal role in childbearing, given human biology

===========

Thinks childbearing can be equal, except that women should get to decide whether they are going to have a child or not, regardless of what the sperm donor may think

Comfortable with the idea that on average
women tend to be a bit smarter than men

———

Comfortable with the idea that among
exceptionally intelligent people men tend to be

Assumes that if women are underrepresented in
an organization or field it's because they aren't
interested in the work, or smart enough

———

Assumes that if men are underrepresented it's
because they aren't interested
or focused enough

Talks about misogyny all the time but has never
heard the word "misandry"

———

Thinks Miss Ogeny and Miss Andry both
sound pretty bossy

Confident that a female-dominated society would be more prosperous, peaceful and just, but that there couldn't possibly be any benefit to having a society dominated by males

———

Confident that a female-dominated society would end up like Venezuela, except overrun with bossy women

Assumes that toxic masculinity is a major problem, but that there couldn't possibly be something called "toxic femininity," unless it meant women who are too tolerant of toxic men

———

Assumes that "toxic masculinity" means men who are afraid of standing up to bossy women

Believes that women are just as strong as men, but men are physically larger and more violent and in need of more social control than women

———

Believes that women are the gentler sex, and need to be protected from men

Thinks the best ways to control men and protect women are chivalry and female modesty

———

Thinks the best methods are gender workshops and making men sit while urinating

Doesn't see that feminism lost the plot when it switched from demanding equality of opportunity to stoking permanent gender war

———

Doesn't see that feminism isn't a plot

Right-wing "incels" who blame
left-wing women for the fact that they are
involuntarily celibate

———————

Left-wing incels who blame right-wing incels
for the fact that they are involuntarily celibate

Women who want men to be less
traditionally masculine but then get irritated
when they aren't ambitious and stoic

———————

Men who want women to be more
traditionally feminine but then can't be
bothered to plan for or support a family

Ostentatiously pious and outspoken church-
going men who regularly cheat on their wives

———————

Ostentatiously pious and outspoken feminist
men who regularly cheat on their wives

Men who think they'll be saved from
#MeToo because they are noisily left-wing,
so rekon there's no point in holding back now

━━━━━━

Men who think they'll be targeted by
#MeToo because they are noisily right-wing,
so rekon there's no point in holding back now

Men confidently mansplaining

━━━━━━

Men confidently mansplaining mansplaining

Fig. IX(a): Limited vocabulary

Fig. IX(b): No words

IX

Drawl, twang, New Yorkese,
Long Islander, New Jerseyan,
Floridian, Upper Midwesterner

═══════════

Mid-Atlantic, vocal fry, upspeak

Thoughts and prayers

═══════════

Allyship

Alternative facts, false equivalence,
problematic, whataboutism,
microaggression, weaponized, triggered

═══════════

Bullshit, same shit,
something's wrong, fuhgeddaboudit,
insult, lock and load, fire when ready

Smirk of privilege

═══════════

Resting bitch face

Limited vocabulary

═══════════

No words

Proud member of the
reality-based community

───────

Facts don't care
about your feelings

Elections have consequences

───────

Suck it, libtards

My body my right

───────

Don't tread on me

Live free or die

—————

No justice, no peace

Wingnuts and cranks

—————

Haters and losers

Swamp cronies

—————

Know-nothings hacks

Snowflake soy boy betas

===

Cis bro chickenhawk cucks

Feminazis

===

Nazis

Smug

===

Mean

Deplorable

═══════════

Nasty

Resistance

═══════════

Patriots

Goldman Sachs

═══════════

Goldman Sachs

Erik D'Amato has worked as a journalist, corporate intelligence operative and media executive on five continents. While based in Central Europe from 1998-2014 he founded a network of news, lifestyle and humor websites spotlighted in the *New York Times*, the *Guardian*, Gawker, and other international media, and earlier was a New York-based writer for *Men's Health* and many other publications. He is on Twitter @erikdamato.

This book was independently published without institutional support or a major media platform, so if you enjoyed it please take the time to let others know about it.

Visit equivalencebook.com to reach the book's Amazon page, where you can leave a review and send copies to friends, or tweet your feedback @TrueEquivalence.

You can also reach the author at mail@erikdamato.com

Printed in Great Britain
by Amazon